THE GODS
*and
Other Beings*

THE GODS
and
Other Beings

*Poems
by
Donald Kuspit*

ZIGGURAT BOOKS
International

The Gods and Other Beings
Copyright ©2010 by Donald Kuspit
Donald Kuspit's Poetry
Copyright © 2010 by Diane Thodos

All rights reserved. Except for brief passages quoted in
a newspaper, magazine, radio, or television program, no
part of this book may be reproduced in any form or by any
means, electronic or mechanical, including photocopying
and recording, or by any information storage and retrieval
system, without permission in writing from the Publisher.

Front cover painting:
Church with a Clock 2009
by Stephen Newton

UK office: 27 St. Quentin House, Fitzhugh Grove,
London SW18 3SE, England
Editorial office: 6 rue Argenterie,
30170 St. Hippolyte du Fort, France
Enquiries: zigguratbooks@orange.fr

Printed by Imprint Digital, Upton Pyne, Exeter

Distributed by Central Books Ltd.
99 Wallis Road, London E9 5LN, England
Tel UK: 0845 458 9911
Fax UK: 0845 459 9912
Tel International: +44 20 8525 8800
Fax International: +44 20 8525 8879
E-mail: orders@centralbooks.com

First Edition

ISBN 978-0-9561038-7-1

Donald Kuspit is one of America's most distinguished art critics. Winner of the prestigious Frank Jewett Mather Award for Distinction in Art Criticism (1983), given by the College Art Association, Professor Kuspit is a Contributing Editor at *Artforum*, *Sculpture*, and *Tema Celeste* magazines, and the editor of *Art Criticism*. He has received fellowships from the Ford Foundation, Fulbright Commission, National Endowment for the Arts, National Endowment for the Humanities, Guggenheim Foundation, and Asian Cultural Council, among other organizations. He has doctorates in philosophy (University of Frankfurt) and art history (University of Michigan), as well as degrees from Columbia University, Yale University, and Pennsylvania State University. He has also completed the course of study at the Psychoanalytic Institute of the New York University Medical Center. Donald Kuspit is Distinguished Professor of Art History and Philosophy at the State University of New York at Stony Brook, and has been the A. D. White Professor-at-Large at Cornell University (1993-98).

Among Donald Kuspit's most recent books are *The Cult of the Avant-Garde Artist* (New York: Cambridge University Press, 1993); *The Dialectic of Decadence* (New York: Stux Press, 1993; reissued, New York: Allworth Press, 2000); *The New Subjectivism: Art in the 1980s* (Ann Arbor: UMI Research Press, 1988; reissued, New York: Da Capo Press, 1993); *Signs of Psyche in Modern and Post-Modern Art* (New York: Cambridge University Press, 1994); *Idiosyncratic Identities: Artists at the End of the Avant-Garde* (New York: Cambridge University Press, 1996); *The Rebirth of Painting in the Late Twentieth Century* (New York: Cambridge University Press, 2000); *Psychostrategies of Avant-Garde Art* (New York: Cambridge University Press, 2000); *Redeeming Art: Critical Reveries* (New York: Allworth Press, 2000); *The End of Art* (New York: Cambridge University Press, 2004). He is also the author of three books of poetry: *Self-Refraction* (1983; visual accompaniment by Rudolf Baranik); *Apocalypse with Jewels in the Distance* (2000; visual accompaniment by Rosalind Schwartz); and *On The Gathering Emptiness* (2004; visual accompaniment by Walter Feldman and Hans Breder).

Diane Thodos is an expressionist artist and art critic who lives in Evanston, Illinois. She is the recipient of a 2002 Pollock-Krasner grant and has exhibited internationally over the span of her 30 year career. She is a former student of Donald Kuspit and the printmaker Stanley William Hayter and has also written numerous artist monograph essays and art criticism for publications including *Art on Paper*, *The New Art Examiner*, *Dialogue Magazine*, and currently the art webzines Artcritical.com and Neotericart.com.

Contents

Introduction by Diane Thodos 1

Foreword 5

The Gods 9

The Devils 53

Anti-climax 57

Death of Narcissus 61

Music of the Spheres 65

Yu Unbound 71

Urweiblichkeit 77

For Louise Bourgeois 83

Introduction

Donald Kuspit's Poetry
by Diane Thodos

Donald Kuspit's poetry has always drawn from the deep well of the Symbolist poetic tradition. In these works memory conjures up myth, desire, regret, and bewilderment, creating an expressive space that captures profound and ineluctable states of mind. Between the longing for transcendence and reflections on mortality these poems are existential meditations which fold time into memory, often discovering emotional spaces which have a depthless silence of feeling. The masterful splitting of poetic lines creates an expressive gap where meaning slips and elides, transporting the mind into unexpected states of awareness. Like a fisherman, the poet casts his line into the sea of his unconscious to recapture the gleanings of primal innocence and wonder. Kuspit unearths the deep eddies and tides where the subconscious flows and where his penetrating and introspective emotions draw the reader into a transcendent journey in search of the self.

Foreword

The Gods and Other Beings: Selected References
by Donald Kuspit

Language itself is influenced by the social repression of certain experiences which do not fit into the structure of a given society; languages differ inasmuch as different experiences are repressed, and hence inexpressible. I leave aside here a quite different problem, that of the possibility of expressing subtle and complex feeling experiences through language, which can be attempted only in poetry.

Erich Fromm, *Greatness and Limitations of Freud's Thought*

At their best...poets seek to remedy the a priori deficiencies of language as an aesthetic medium by undoing its prior meanings and by conferring something like a bodily substance upon it, however their actions violate the way in which language is used to functioning...

Words thus manipulated demand that we treat them as an aesthetic medium and not as we do in routine discourse, that we attend them rather than going through them once we have deciphered their code; each formal group of them wants to be seen centripetally rather than centrifugally, as a filled and present center and not as one that has been emptied out and turned into an absence. We pretty nearly can heft them and, consequently, come to pay tribute to their innate powers that overwhelm the distance between the arbitrary relation between signifier and signified that governs the normal use of language. Far from arbitrary, they persuade us of their corporeal indispensability.

Murray Krieger, *Arts on the Level: The Fall of the Elite Object*

Having assimilated much of the Not-Me, the child at last accommodates his vision to the vision of others. Poets, we can assume, are children who have *assimilated* more than the rest of us, and yet somehow have *accommodated* less, and so have won through the crisis of adolescence without totally decentering.

Harold Bloom, *Figures of Capable Imagination*

The Gods
I. to XXXIV.

I.

they are more ancient
 than words,
and more turbulent
 and innocent, unalterably.
too wild to be reined in
 by recognition,
to be tamed by thought,
 branded by consciousness.
too infinite to be broken
 on the rack of reason
however stretched out of shape
 into ideas.

when their rambling silence
 casts its shadow
in human speech
 meaning no longer miscarries.
trusted,
 they freshen human existence,
making it unconscious
 of itself.
wonder re-asserts its rights,
 bringing the gods
into careless view again,
 hesitantly given by the sky
dressing them in light.

 they precipitate out of the invisible,
instantly dissolving
 into incomprehensibility,
emptying the perception
 impinging on them,
reclaiming their innocence
 by unburdening themselves

of the beings
        they created when they began time.
they renew the indifference
                of eternity
whenever they make
        no human difference.

II.

burdened, by the endless
                        misunderstanding of being,
erupting from the beginning,
                            beginning again and again,
as though there was no end
                        to measure,
no final form to the despair
                        lingering in wisdom,
the wordlessness of your forms
                            giving my words courage.

give again,
          that i never need again,
transcendence staring me
                      in the face at twilight,
when the wind conquers
                      the skyscrapers,
leaps towards your temples
                      in myths,
where the cities collapse
                      into pastorals,
and death emerges,
                witless and directionless,
its arrows bent
          by the silence
which triumphs over all.

III.

there was nothing,
                then the small something
you gave unbidden,
                storming the silence
with your thunder
                until it rained wonder,
raising questions
                that encompassed vastness.

undoing the blankness
                of the sky
with clouds of consciousness,
                you open the way
beyond death,
                my hymns burrowing
into the bosom
                of your beyond,
huddling in the shroud
                of wisdom.

IV.

more whimsical than impulse,
                          and more blunt,
your silence puts words
                to shame,
your calm embarrasses
                consciousness.
you never fail me
            however much I fail myself,
tempted by despair,
           as though to unburden wisdom
of care,
    memory of meaning.
whirligigs abound
           in the stillness,
marking time
       with their movement,
solemn as the flames
          that arch the sky,
the eye passing through
           to pure light
filtered by the infinite
           innocence of your indifference,
blinding me with its radiance.
                   grant me insight into the stars
before I lose sight,
         that I finally love the darkness
that is greater than them,
            and you.

V.

words have lost their whimsy,
                         and all that is left is death,
and hints of gods
           unbroken on the rack of time,
unchurned by the chaos
               abiding in the inevitable.

their patience is the only power.
                      wisdom comes
with the loss of words,
            seeing beyond their futility
to unbroken silence,
              ignoring their broken promises
for the final innocence.

                 emptiness grows luminous
as eyes falter
          flying with angels beyond the sky,
where nothing is left to be seen,
                fate at last free
to drag me unresisting
              to the gods in my grave.

VI.

still in need of me,
                    as the need for you
grows in me,
            for we need each other
to live on
        now that we no longer
need words
        to live on,
now that we can only
                grow in silence,
never outgrowing
            each other
so long as we are able
                to grow unseen.

do not fool me
             as all my other loves have,
do not fail me
            the way i fail myself,
do not abandon me
                to meaninglessness
the way words have.
                    your sky has gone gray,
but i find you
            in the hint of light
lingering unseen,
                a seductive fossil
of feeling
        i find preserved between
the faded pages
                of childhood feeling.

VII.

the gods have lost
                their recklessness,
their intensity exhausted
                      in rituals of images
and ideas,
        their altars cluttered
with tarnished trophies
                of intricate thought,
their bodies embalmed
                    in manufactured enigmas.
o once again to find
                a fresh sky
beyond the cross
            of consciousness,
even the more miraculous
                    sky unclouded
by the unconscious.
                unadulterated eternity
in a flower,
          the sacred freshly blossoming
in the immensity
            of its color's innocence,
feeling no longer forcefed
                  by longing
for the illimitable
            but content
with the incomprehensibly
                intimate,
simple seeing
        of simple being,
unseen gods spreading
              like pollen
from the plenitude
            of simplicity.

look with the outward eye,
                        for the inward looking
eye has become vain,
                        knowing what it sees
before it sees it,
                        so that it can never truly see it.
look without wanting
                        to know,
without mutilating
                        with meaning.
only the simply seen
                        breeds unknown gods,
no other kind being known
                        today.
only in life distilled
                        into immaculate immediacy
can gods be seen,
                        if never again reckless
enough to power life,
                        let alone last forever.

VIII.

the gods remain good,
                wisdom pouring forth
from their tears,
          their eyes once again all seeing,
replenished by innocence.
                purged of the world
their plenitude becomes evident
                    in their silence.
let the myth of them remain
              when all is finished,
so the sky can be burnished
              by their presence,
that my eyes have a resting place
                of wonder,
untouched by the indifference
              of death.
no shadows to fear
          when their light comes unbidden,
a thread of light
          leading me out of the labyrinth
of longing
       into the pastoral space of myth,
with its miracles
          of memory.

IX.

you too were broken
                         on the rack of wonder,
the passing of it all
                      into the problematic,
the noble dissolved
                  in the trivial,
the sky crushed
               by its own emptiness.
temples no longer
                 live in the clouds,
breathing the mist
                of my longing,
the truth no longer
                   pours from the cornucopia
of consciousness,
                eyes no longer lift themselves
in devotion,
            their wisdom the empty stare
of the eyeless statue.
                you have worn out
your welcome in the world,
                      but you are always
welcome in my world
                of words,
which like you
            will only be remembered
by strangers
              terrorized by the final silence.

X.

we have become strangers
                              to ourselves,
like the dead.
                but stuck between eternity
and time we are neither
                        dead nor alive
but hopelessly naïve,
                      birds that must always return
to the ark of memory
                      for no fresh land is ever in sight.
the only freshness is our flight,
                            for earth spoiled
by impiety
           can no longer see the sky.

we must breed
              our own destinies
with words,
           for they alone can break
our fall when
              our wings finally falter,
dropping us
            into the meaninglessness.
there at last we wonder
                    with no net
of consciousness
            to catch us
before we become completely
                            unconscious.

XI.

death is the foundation
                         of the world,
but you need no
                foundation to build
yourselves.
          living in silence
in temples of thought
                you rise
majestically in moods
                  of innocence,
your absence
         all the freshness
i need,
     all the serenity
i could want,
         all the wonder
i can see.
        the desert of time
blossoms
         with passing memories,
but you abide,
              pagan cacti
of prickly consciousness
                  storing up
all the water
        left of life.

XII.

you keep finding me
                where there is no self left to find,
my body huddled
              in a corner of my consciousness
like a homeless myth.
                      i am the bone
that is the secret
            of your survival,
the wordless thought
              that is your flesh.
the world shreds you
              with its suffering,
but you abide
          in the bleeding silence,
inarticulate as wisdom.
                    wonders will cease
when you are deciphered;
                  warrior shadows
will overrun the world.
                you will become
the outspoken emptiness
              enduring in stone,
raw as the ruins
        of ancient thought
in mutable memory,
                  the death that finally triumphs
when the self
        falls back on its fading memories.

XIII.

given that your words
                came unwillingly
and uneasily,
        and no longer support
the sky,
    twisting in on itself
in innocent
        incomprehensibility,
they continue
        to give sense
to my wonder.
            whimsically spiraling upward
as they drift downward,
                  it meets their meaning halfway,
breaking their fall
        in a blur of consciousness.
finally become ineffable,
            along with your invisibility,
they crumble
        in clouds of consciousness
and icarian lightning.

            stars stop spinning,
and stumble over shadow,
              spreading comfortably
over the cosmos,
        settling a shroud of silence
over its broken spire.
           ashes of nuance
drift in the emptiness,
        reminding me of gods
who may have been.

XIV.

you became flesh,
                         or is it the brittle bone
of memory,
            resurrected as the myth
of higher consciousness?
                         maggots of meaning
grow in your rot,
               giving death a sense
it does not deserve,
                  in fear of its senselessness.
o folly
     of our self-deception,
death is not as far
               as heaven,
but as close
          as the next breath,
as intimate
          as every passing moment.

cast your sheen
               on death's ghastliness
that it look more seductive
                      than life,
as though death alone
                could satisfy
every desire forbidden in life.
                       liars all,
you are the dirty dreams
               of death,
as though it could lead
               to childhood heights
of happiness
         rather than fall through
the bottom of time.

                       eternity never existed,
even in miracles of memory.
                                no ecstasy
of illusion
           can satisfy the desire for immortality.

XV.

i raise a spiral column
                      of longing into your dome,
entering the space of consciousness
                              you inhabit
in serene invisibility.
                  beyond it there is only
the vacancy of meaning
                        that is the common sky.
clouds form vowels
                of hesitant feeling,
cabalistic inklings
                of your presence,
but your silence remains aloof.

                                to see you is to see
my death,
        for you are death in the disguise of infinity,
death adorned
              with the pomp of mystery,
death's inevitability
                    made innocent in the marvel
of your existence.
                you miraculously defy time's gravity,
but you cannot defy
                the miracle of my longing for you,
drawing you to my grave
                  like flies to sour honey.

gild fate with your glory,
                      and let your incestuous loves
distract the mind
              from its betrayal by life.

XVI.

your death
           was as brilliant
as ever,
      gilded with lilies
of memory
           and bolts of thought,
seeping through
           the darkness
with myth's
         precision.
o your ancient
          fortitude
has broken down
           on the cross.
your ashes
        avalanche
with the thunder
          of shadow,
your mountain
         collapsed
under the weight
          of the emptiness,
you gone forever
           in the fervor
of silence.
      but be with me
as i anoint
        my own death,
king of me
        as forgetfulness
is king of you.

XVII.

the gods howled,
                alone at last,
with the birds,
                shedding their wings
like leaves
        yet gaining height
with every loss.
                circling together
in an aura of wind,
                suddenly mingling
in the inevitable wonder
                outpacing mind,
reaching where words fail,
                limited by lasting silence
piercing
        to the quick of time.

so we flew pierced
                by light,
reaching the depths
                of darkness
to recover our senses
                in the immediate,
racing in the current
                of clouds
idealizing our nakedness,
                until we too outpaced
time with our intimacy,
                and contentment.

XVIII.

silence is the crime
                of their consciousness,
killing meaning
           with its immensity.
they make themselves known
                  through outworn miracles
bespeaking the freshness
             of their inevitability.
we feel their invisibility
             when we outlast our words,
feeding on themselves
           when there is no world
left to feed on,
         and the sundial no longer
casts a shadow.

         words are the leavings of life,
labored crumbs of consciousness
                 easily scattered
by the unconscious,
           but the gods are the remains
of death,
      visible when there is nothing left
to remember,
         only the ecstasy of enigma
when their light
           shines in every corner of our blindness,
outlasting the everlasting void
                for a lingering moment,
humbling us with the purity
             that restores innocence
of vision
     when there is nothing left to envision.

XIX.

i unburdened myself to you,
                         and when there was nothing left
to burden you with,
            i burdened myself with you,
carrying you through realms
                 of conscious disbelief
to unconscious belief.
             once a comfortable nest of meanings,
my consciousness fell apart
               on the rack of doubt
triggered by a wonder
            that outgrew its restraints.
ideas become weeds
            along ancient highways of thought,
which became byways of life,
              detours of meaning
on a meaningless map of mind.
               so i carried you as far
as my crippled consciousness could,
                   through all the wastelands
of thought,
       safely arriving at the paradise
of thoughtlessness.
             my agony built an altar
in the ruins of my consciousness,
                   so i could worship you freely,
you being the first and last fruits
              of my life,
grateful at last for its gift,
               which you and your love are.

XX.

my wonder left you
                breathless
as a vacuum,
          mired in the black space
of memory.
          rummaging through death
i found you in ramshackle
                constellations,
flamboyantly innocent
                with light,
idiosyncratically ideal
                despite the emptiness.
pursued through pathos,
                you were more protean
than passion,
          changing shape at will
to spite time.
          again and again your enigma
exhausted itself,
                but my wonder was your fountain
of youth.
        blindly feeling my way
through your invisibility,
                almost stopped
by the steepness of your silence,
                    i finally reached
beyond the limits
          of my consciousness,
and held you fast
              in the thin air of my love,
embracing your echo
              in the distance
opening my eyes
          to your remoteness.

XXI.

forgotten at last,
                you are fuller than you ever were
in the embrace
        of my innocence,
when there was no need
                for words.
only unalloyed wonder.
                now doubt has dramatized
your presence,
        suddenly poignant with regret,
and archaic emptiness.
                i toy with the thought of you,
intemperately aware
        of your unawareness
of death,
      even as you breathe it in with every silence.
breathe me in,
        that we become ghosts
of each other,
        complete ourselves
with the other's
        incompleteness.

XXII.

comforting mirages,
                lounging in the
limitless heaven
                our envy has created for them—
but they're apocalyptic jockeys,
                lightning flashes
reveling in the sky
                like willful ghosts,
heralded by the fierceness
                of their silence,
and foretold in a blinding moment
                of fear,
more reckless and restless
                than they are.
insight menaces sight,
                turning the transparent opaque
at the moment of their rebirth
                in memory,
coldblooded myths
                given a new lease on life
by my hotblooded wonder.
                o that the monsters
would disappear as suddenly
                as they reappeared,
awakened from death
                by my wish for their wisdom.
but they leave me
                with the burden of my disbelief,
for there is no wisdom
                about life in the afterlife.
the devastation wrought
                by my disappointment signals
a fresh start for the sky,
                freeing it forever of the gods

clouding it with their obscurity,
                                    finally as clear and peaceful
as my consciousness
                withdrawn into its limits.

XXIII.

the gods no longer bless,
                        they're bored
with the godless,
                abandoning them
in the emptiness
                of meaning at the end
of the colorless rainbow
                        of their consciousness,
hanging like a sickle
                  over the abundance.
burnishing the beauty
                of the sky,
the gods carouse
              on dissolving clouds,
no irony
        soiling their divinity.
virginal in all their lusts,
                    fate merrily playing
in their mindless pleasures,
                        their longing unspent
however often spent.
                  the tightminded wisdom
of the godless
              has left them in the lurch,
trembling
          in the ruins of their thought,
isolated in the castles
                  of consciousness
they fortified against
                the unconscious,
where gods are spawned
                    by limitless longing,
glowworms joyously spawned
                        by the darkness left

when the mind
                has finally been exhausted by enigma.

XXIV.

the damned are everywhere,
                               willing and unwilling,
shortsighted and brokenhearted,
                               their emptiness
blossoming in their eyes,
                         their consciousness
the coy chatter
                 of pontificating staleness,
truth forgotten
                 in words that have lost the freshness
that made it ineffable.
                       the toiling angels
have fled the shadows
                     limping in the light
no longer enabling
                 the enigma.
the gods have become blindspots
                             in the vacuum of vision,
their lost wisdom the aftertaste
                       of death.
o that they be converted
                     by my consciousness
into the mirage that remains
                       in the desert
that damns me with its silence,
                         broken only
by the wind that sifts
                     the sand in its hourglass.

XXV.

the gods have lost
                their freshness,
cosmic dust
          falling on the earth,
a mystery gone bankrupt,
                      no longer found
even in shadow,
              unearthed from the emptiness.
dwindling to an unhappy few
                  in fantasy,
not worth the yearning unbound,
                    no longer
the succulent fruit
            of the ripest senses,
no longer corrupting
              my consciousness
with revelation,
            majestically impinging
in the darkness turned inside out,
                      in the luminous immediacy
of their fullness.
            they've returned to darkness,
insistent with inevitability,
                      beyond recall except in illusion,
myth that gives meaning
              to what has lost living meaning.
there the gods appear
            like nocturnal emissions,
ghostly spurts ecstatically lamed,
                      unexpectedly limping
through my loins,
            suddenly convulsed
with unforgettable feeling for them,
                        my flesh as mystical

as theirs,
> however faceless and impotent they remain
in my mind,
>> as though still unborn and virginal.

XXVI.

they broke and ran,
                falling over each other,
stumbling in the emptiness,
                    myth left over
from longing
          the atmosphere they breathe,
thinning as i reach
              their heights,
leaving me to breathe
              their nothingness.
once i held them as firmly
                  as Samson held
the jawbone of an ass,
                once they were as colorful
as Joseph's coat,
              once they burned the bushes
into supernatural light,
                once they were constellations
of stars that condensed
            their power.
now they are buried alive
              in the pomp of ritual,
ungraspable except
           when i fall in wingless words,
disappearing like dew
              before i hit bottom.

XXVII.

they were once my living ancestors,
                                          now they dance on my grave
with other ghosts of memory,
                          living only in poems
as desiccated as falling leaves,
                            crumbling into dusty words
before they reach unconsciousness.
                              let their brittleness fertilize
a fresh consciousness
                    that i once again may live among the gods,
their enigma restored
                in eyes opened by love,
no longer in need of memory
                        to tend their presence,
but face to face with them
                      in a paradise of wonder,
a clearing in tangled thoughts
                        of immortality.

XXVIII.

the moon's nipple
                is not as sweet
as the sun's nipple,
                    and the gods have become moons
around a planet grown
                dark with disbelief.
the succulence
            has gone out of light,
hanging static in the falling sky.
                      the gods no longer rise
like unexpected whirlwinds
                in a desert of words,
but limp in the silence
                that builds up
around consciousness
              and buries it alive,
turning the gods
            into cosmic dust again,
so they can no longer speak
                  in the tongues of nature.
but the unconscious
            eagerly sucks the sour milk
from the moon's nipple,
                for it always finds death
more nourishing
            and fresher than life.

XXIX.

the gods grate,
            as all ways to wonder do,
whether mirage
            or memory.
the radioactivity in darkness,
                      the innocence in nothingness,
cacti of consciousness
            in deserts of feeling,
the silence unveiled
            after words fail,
the freshness after the storm
                of shadow,
the elated futility
            of the evening sun,
the budding grace
            in the dead sky—
back to the beginning
            when every day is a dead-end,
back into the dead-end
                when there are no more fresh starts.

XXX.

time retreats from the gods
                              as they retreat from me,
even as my wonder begets them,
                                   as death beget me.
no regrets remain to comfort
                              the emptiness,
no spoils of meaning to refresh
                              the staleness,
no delights of thought to sweeten
                              the silence,
no panic to arouse possibility.
                              the gods are found
in loss,
     like everything that is actual because it lingers.

XXXI.

the gods embraced
                each other like shadows
after sunset,
        and then dawn arose like myth,
remaking the world
           after memory.
there was no afterglow
                of wisdom,
no final word of glory
                for the forgotten,
no bemoaning
        what could never be remembered.
o bitterness
        of the first beginning,
and the many others
            that never began,
always beginning
           where there is waste
of words,
      always the fresh start
of silence,
        always fulfillment
in the cosmic chatter
              indecipherable
in its bowels,
        the urge regurgitated
in its stuttering.
          i too will find my fate
in the forgotten,
           beginning again
where there can never
              be an end.

XXXII.

when all the memories
                    have died,
then gods are reborn,
                    more concise
than their statues,
                    more durable
than the stone
                    that hardens them
into visibility,
                    more immaculate
than any idea quarried
                    from the mind
unblemished by the world.
                    words recover innocence
baptized in their silence,
                    instincts lose urgency
in their innocence,
                    space regains limitlessness
in the shadow they cast
                    on time.
again the senses become angels
                    moving along the ladder
leading to their love,
                    again every detail of nature
is shaped
        by their luminous meaning,
grace before the fall
                    restored in their myth-making light.
my consciousness crumbles
                    so that i can meet
them in the darkness
                    they no longer leave,
will o' the wisps
                    spontaneously generated

by the phosphorescent decay
                        in the dreary unconscious.

XXXIII.

mad as the birds
                that conquer the silence
with their swiftness,
                      delirious as wisdom,
merry with fathomless
                  delight at being,
beckoning in the light
                  that lingers in darkness,
as everlasting as the darkness
                  is limitless,
wonder at last liberated
                  from empty longing,
spontaneously generated
                  by death
the way death
            is spontaneously generated
by thought,
            each taking the measure of meaning
with its own kind
                of immeasurability.
they were revealed
                in a miracle of consciousness,
but even more miraculous
                  was their power
to change hate into love
                  in the unconscious,
to change falling stars
                  into rising suns in memory.

XXXIV.

prodrome,
           then the bitter gods
tainted by time,
                yawning in my head,
needing no brain
             to know the inevitable,
adorable in their simplicity,
                      pollinating
the silence
        with their sensitivity,
bleeding the sun dry,
              its light spilling
from their veins,
             until they too are colorless,
withered flowers
               pressed between the pages
of a book of forgotten wisdom,
                    where they crumble
into unconsciousness.
                then the nausea
unleashed by their loss,
                    the terror of timelessness lost,
even to memory,
           unthinkable except
when panic
        gives them presence.

The Devils
I. to II.

I.

    they were as excruciating
                            as wisdom,
    and just as worthless.
                            remembering them
    glistening in the streets
                            like stale raindrops,
    they slipped into the chaos
                            of sound
    that enveloped space,
                            squeezing it dry
    of all memory,
                   until eternity stood stark,
    soliciting me
               with its emptiness.

    words came uncalled for,
                            for there was nothing
    but them to fill the gap,
                            and they widened it.
    between you and me
                            the succubi of the senses
    ran wild with wonder,
                            stripping limits from the loins
    of light
          to reveal the immodest darkness.

II.

briskly horny,
                you were plagued by the angels
who pecked at your rears,
                        reminding you of all you lost
when you shat in the mouth
                      of the lord,
leaving your aftertaste
                in his bliss.
you put words
              in place of his sovereign silence,
soiling the timeless
                with tempting chatter,
wrecking wonder
              with seductive immediacy,
fouling purity
          with animal urgency.

guide me through
                this underworld of the everyday,
but keep your butt
                out of my upperworld,
where no bodies
            can bewilder the wordless mind.

Anti-climax

anti-climax

trapped between starlight
                         and sunlight
was light that would never
                         be named,
angelic innocence
                in permanent amnesia
of timelessness.
                no-person of death
swathed in manic clouds,
                        wings unfettered
by boundaries,
                trespassing the unknowable.
cast out of heaven,
                  i envied their wonder,
their ease of flight
                hinting at the void,
where there was only
                  fearless waiting,
the promise of grace
                     become the sleeplessness
of knowing,
           the helplessness of hope.

Death of Narcissus

death of narcissus

death rose up,
               righting itself
in the mirror,
               self-righteous with shimmering
inevitability,
               undefeated by the lack
of light.
      i mirrored it
before we met
               in the nightmare
of my self-knowing,
               blurring us
into each other's substance.

               o phantom lover,
remember me
        for my embrace
of your indifference,
               mythologize me
into immutable memory,
               free in the fathomless silence
of reflection,
             absorbed at last by absence,
unmistakably other
             yet true to myself.
o grave of all meaning,
               your solemn emptiness
adds fullness to the mystery
               breathing the last light:
let me find rest in the bosom
               of your smile.

Music of the Spheres
I. to III.

I.

brutalized by silence,
      the gods beckoned,
surly with time.
     o that the will to wonder
would recover
     from their savagery,
and innocence reign
      once again in words,
purity of intention
      liberating them from longing
for the inconceivable,
      seductive in the silence.
let there be no sky,
     only the labor of emptiness,
sucking all into the pause
      between the notes,
the music suddenly hesitant
      as the spheres spin
out of control,
     like words that linger with wonder.

II.

no gods were left
                in the silence,
only the unfinished wonder,
                        wandering
with the empty-eyed gaze
                    of homeless angels,
if being on their own
                is homelessness.
the sky emerged once more
                      with the briskness of light,
the gray that voiced the void
                      retreating from recognition,
until all was a golden glow
                    of unfurled wings,
freshening the air
              with their polish.
however high my words flew
                      they felt like angels falling,
even though the angels flew
                    faster than words could fall.

III.

they were uncaring
                in their calm,
shedding shadow
                as they raised my eyes,
becoming more enigmatic
                as they became pupillary.
my eyes circled with them,
                becoming as majestic;
leavened by their light,
                they became symmetrical music.
silence unfurled
                in the music,
breathing the wind
                of the rhythm,
until wonder dwindled
                into memory
when dawn revealed
                the world's indifference.

Yu Unbound
I. to IV.

I.

nature is famished,
                    and you feed her art,
restoring the elements
                    to enigma,
a blessing in color,
                    tumultuous with feeling,
flowing with the freshness
                    of glaciers and lava,
the extremes meeting
                    in light,
the primordial truth
                    unfettered in the force
of their mating,
                    hell and heaven at last one
in a primal scene.

the fury crackling
                    in the distance,
sounds amazed
              by their own silence
in the vastness,
                    the force ruptured
by its own solemnity,
                    ruthless at last with the insistence
of chance,
              auratic traces of time
in chaotic motion,
                    awed by the suddenness
into mystical whimsy,
                    passion unstoppably dervishing
in her ruthless senses.

II.

you on fire,
            unearthed in your ruby lust,
liberated from the underground
                          of your exploding senses,
the force of unfurled emotions
                        in your naked colors,
tumbling over themselves
                        in timeless space,
the invisible mutating
                  with nameless power,
the formless impacted
                  in cells of consciousness,
swarming in the turbulent silence
                          more grandiose
than the gods ever were,
                  the final spasm
as lasting
          as their forgotten freshness.

III.

your body is the breath
                         of lava,
out of control
               in avalanching colors,
forming a rainbow
                        above barren consciousness,
where eternity hibernates,
                           waiting for a new spring
of passion to renew your flesh
                          in elemental art.
crystallized motion
                  calms the saturated senses,
but your eye never loses
                    its orgasmic nerve,
spasming out of sight
                  into glacial silence
rhythmically melting
                  the lingering shadows
into all-embracing light.
                        the primal scene endures
in the unforeseen unity
                  of ever-changing
feeling and matter.

IV.

you run hot and cold,
                        but never quietly,
your nature as elemental
                        as mythical nature.
the force of nature
                        is the force of your passion,
now frozen in glaciers,
                        now molten in lava,
now underground
                        in the scenery of the unconscious,
now conscious
                        in crystallized color.
turquoise is eternal,
                        ruby is the wine of life
crushed from the grapes
                        of fresh senses,
yours always blossoming
                        with new flowers of feeling.
words exhaust themselves,
                        becoming as motionless
as death,
                        but your nature lives forever,
inexhaustible matter
                        in erotic motion,
the protean grandeur
                        of the instinctive goddess.

Urweiblichkeit
I. to III.

I.

face adrift
        like a wayward dune,
body a Pompeian corpse,
                blankness bleeding
from your eyes,
        brittle straw hair
crowning a shapeless smile,
                breasts slumped
on a collapsed belly,
                o tell me about the lovers
who once lay across
            its boundlessness,
bathing in your pulchritude,
                a fountain of youth
for those willing
        to pay the price.
my words will restore
            your flesh
to virginal freshness,
            firm your nipples
with nuance,
        cover you with a softening veil
of care,
    hide the smell of death
with their perfume.
            once again your touch
will be a blessing,
        if only in a myth of my making.
once again your lust
            will make the commonplace captivating,
as my love
        will make you uncommon once again.
the world fades into inconsequence
                when i make love to you,

if only with words,
>for my flesh is as faded as yours,
and words, however overused,
>>never become as useless
as flesh finally does,
>however alive with memory.

II.

ah yes, woman,
>   one of the seven blunders
of the world,
>   nature's clumsy fatality
at its most naïve,
>   the instincts' bad joke
on divinity,
>   matrix of every stillborn meaning,
leveler of consciousness.
>   big lie of the limitless
in orgasmic intimacy,
>   fake freshness
of feeling in glamour,
>   cosmetic fantasy
covering your flesh
>   with make-believe mystery.
only the spoiled brat
>   dares mock your vanity,
holding up the mirror
>   that strips the figleaf
of fantasy
>   from your nakedness,
exposing the falseness
>   of your mystery.
yours is not the fairest
>   of all cosmic forms,
but the most deceptive
>   form of death,
the most treacherous
>   form of time.

III.

eve, you were once
                brilliant gold,
now tarnished with memory,
                          florid in words.
lust amused us,
            irony spoiled innocence.
weeds of wisdom
                grew from the ruins
of your flesh,
            stale from suffering.
they wanted for nothing,
                      and it came fullblown
from the swollen silence,
                      carcass of my consciousness.
o become primal rib again,
                    that we renew
our vows in the body
                that existed before
the world began
                and time outran our love.

For Louise Bourgeois

for louise bourgeois

on the last climb
               the first consciousness arrives
when the eye touches
               the sky's tip.
clouds crest
          in waves of wonder,
and spray angels
             on the shores of shadow.
wisdom appears
             in the wordless color,
and the body becomes
               the grace of silence.
art guarantees sanity,
                 but innocence guarantees
immortality.
           find your childhood again
in the changing seasons
               of memory.